Self-Care for Black Women

A Black Woman's Guide to Boost Confidence,
Attract Success and Overcome the Inner Critic
with Empowering Affirmations, Inspirational
Quotes & Important Life Lessons

Destiny Smith

i

Destiny Smith

Destiny Smith

Table of Contents

Your Secret Gift #1

Get My Next Book

"Self-Care for Black Women - Part 2"

(Free for a limited time)

For a limited time, and as a "Thank you" for purchasing this book, you can be added to our "Book 2 Launch List" for free so you get the second book of this series when it gets published (This book will be priced at $24.99 and I guarantee it will be a great read). Simply visit the URL below and follow the instructions. You'll be the first to get it.

Visit here:

lindahillbooks.com/women

Scan QR Code:

Your Secret Gift #2

Get the Audio Version for Free

If you would like to get the audio version of this book so you can read along or listen while you are in the car, walking around, or doing other things, you're in luck. For a limited time, I've provided a link that will allow you to download this audiobook for FREE. (This offer may be removed at any time).

Step 1: Go to the URL below.

Step 2: Sign up for the 30-day free-trial membership (You may cancel at any time after, no strings attached)

Step 3: Listen to the audiobook

Visit here:

lindahillbooks.com/womenpromo

Scan QR Code:

Introduction

You're a woman, you're black, and there's nothing wrong with that.

Black is beautiful, strong, and above all, resilient. A woman is outspoken, graceful, and confident. You are all of these things, even if it doesn't feel that way. Sometimes, it helps to have those affirmations when certain questions arise. What questions pop up, you might ask? Well, there are times when you may ask yourself who you are? Where do you belong? What are you allowed to do?

Media from all different platforms are out there saying what black women should be and how to act. As a black woman, you might be fighting against the stereotypes that have been set in place for centuries. It's a challenge that can overall make you feel hurt and frustrated. Your every move may feel judged and scrutinized. You may feel like you can't talk to whoever you want and love whoever you want.

But that's why this book is here, to reassure you that you can be whoever and whatever you want to be.

You deserve to be happy. You deserve a good life. You deserve love. Your dreams are valid, and you should pursue them. And don't let anyone tell you that you can't, even yourself.

But where do you start?

In your mind.

It can transform your life. All you need to do is change how you think and see how drastically your life can change. Shifting your mindset from negative to positive is a lot easier with affirmations. These phrases help reconfigure your subconsciousness and reaffirm that you are indeed what you say you are.

Positive affirmations are incredible. They can boost your mood, confidence, and self-esteem. This boost in good vibes helps build resilience against the negativity you face every day.

Do you desire a happier, more fulfilling life?

Do you want to be free of the stereotypical cage that you are in?

Do you want to be confident, happy, find love, and have a more positive outlook on life?

If so, then it's time you used this power of repetition to rewrite your thought pattern, habits, beliefs, and ideals to reflect the life you want to have. I won't tell you that your life will instantaneously change just like magic, but what I can assure you is once you incorporate these thoughts and sayings in your life, you will be a different person.

How could I possibly know this, and yet I don't know or understand what you are going through?

If you're worried that you're going through this alone,

don't worry! I'll be here to cheer you on and give you a story or two. But above all you are not alone, and just like those who embraced the power of affirmations, you can change your reality. The affirmations listed here are meant to turn you into the powerful black woman you are, whether you believe you are her or not because we do.

There's no right or wrong way to read through these affirmations. They are categorized so you can easily get to the ones you need whenever you need them. If you need a confidence boost, jump into the confidence section and get the morale boost you need. Jump into whatever section you are struggling with as they give you the help you need for that area.

Let's get into it.

CHAPTER ONE

Affirmation Power: Think, Say, Be

"Toni's Talk: When you invest in yourself, you have instant credibility with your biggest critic...you! As soon as you let doubt creep in---you lose that investment. Make a daily commitment to assess your worth with positive affirmations and watch your investment grow."
— *C. Toni Graham*

We all have two sides, a good one, and an inner critic. The good side is encouraging, loving, and caring, while the inner critic is just that, a critic. She criticizes your thoughts and constantly has you second-guessing who you are. You would think that the good side would be winning, but you are wrong.

We are stuck in a constant tug of war with our positive and negative thoughts, and unfortunately, the negative thoughts are winning. Staying positive-minded in this day and age is becoming harder and harder. Everyone has an opinion, even your inner critic, and because it's so ingrained in us, we take what it says to be true. We forget that we can choose not to listen. After listening to our inner critic discourage us for so long, we develop habits and behaviors that are not good for us. When you have been told you are not beautiful for so long, you start believing it.

However, it's time to silence your inner critic, and a great way to do so is through the power of affirmations. Repeatedly telling yourself that you are beautiful, confident, and a winner is the best way to silence this nagging inner voice. Because guess what? You are all of those things! So this should be easy, right?

Not so fast. To silence your inner critic, you need to be conscious of what you are listening to. After all, the wolf you feed is the wolf that wins. That is why affirmations are so powerful.

So, what are affirmations?

An affirmation is a statement meant to initiate self-change in the person using them. They help you focus your attention and thoughts throughout the day. As such, they serve as sources of inspiration and reminders and have the potential to help promote positive and self-sustained change. When we are feeling good and have a friendly attitude, our lives run smoothly. This is because we are producing positive vibes which attract positive things, such as health, love, peace, confidence, and more. Similarly, when we feel down and have a negative attitude, we engage in self-destructive behaviors that result in negative outcomes. This is when we have lots of interpersonal drama, financial hardships, stress, and more.

The Benefits Behind Affirmations

Telling yourself you are strong, beautiful, or awesome can seem bizarre, and you might be wondering if it's a waste of time, but the human mind is a fascinating thing. It organizes your thoughts and influences your habits and behaviors. It characterizes, defines, places, and explains the energy you feel based on your attentions and experiences. So, if you chant something repeatedly, you will end up believing and becoming it. Basically, if you acknowledge it, you can achieve it.

You have probably heard people say that to live a better, more positive life; you need to speak it into existence. Well, it's true. This simple philosophy is what affirmations are based on. By consistently repeating these positive statements, you are restructuring your subconscious to tone down your inner critic, stay positive, and set yourself up to attain what you desire.

A study in the Journal of Social Cognitive and Affective Neuroscience utilized MRI imaging to reveal how self-affirmation triggers your mind's reward centers. According to the study, positive statements such as "I love myself" lit up the same neural pathways that respond to pleasurable experiences. Additionally, these neural circuits also dampen pain, improve your moods and keep calm in the face of adversity.

In the beginning, our brain's main purpose was to keep us alive. So, it evolved to make quick snap decisions about important things such as food and safety, not spend hours making rigorous analytical observations about everything that's happening. This means that it created shortcuts to solve issues that lead to cognitive biases. These are the beliefs we have and hold to be absolute, even with no proof.

Recognize any of these:

The tendency of novices to overestimate their skill while experts underestimate them. This effect is referred to as the Dunning-Kruger Effect.

The inclination to see more of and believe more of what confirms your beliefs. So, if you believe you are not good enough, you think that everyone else thinks so and when you fail, you see this as proof that you are not enough. This is referred to as cognitive bias.

Noticing more of something once you see it. For instance, if you get a new car, you suddenly start seeing that car model everywhere. This is known as observational selection bias.

These cognitive biases are shortcut neural pathways your brain makes to avoid thinking through and analyzing everything happening. This is because they take time and can be exhausting, so your brain creates these shortcuts.

The magic behind affirmations is that they hijack these pathways to reconstruct your thought process. By repeating these phrases, you convince your brain that you are loved, you will get that job, you are confident, and so on. Soon enough, your mind believes it and subconsciously searches for signs to make this true. When it does, it will present the sign to your conscious mind. Think of it this way: by saying that you are loved, you convince your mind that you are loved, and you start noticing instances of people showing you love.

An affirmation is basically a nudge in the positive direction, and practicing them activates the areas of your brain that make you happy.

Benefits of affirmations

Positive affirmations allow you to stay positive and

determine the tone of your emotional life. They are the good things you say about your emotions, career, love life, family, and everything else. Basically, you are saying what you want to see happen in your life regardless of what's going on right now. They are more than mere phrases; they are your identity. They become your thoughts, habits, and ideals. Some think this is all an enormous waste of time; after all, how can repeating phrases over and over change your future? Others see this as wishful thinking.

But if you think of this as a workout, you realize that just like doing 20 pushups a day can help you tone your arms, your positive affirmations are helping your mind maintain a positive outlook on life. Think of them as mental exercises to reprogram your mind, shut down your inner critic and help you learn to accept yourself. Affirmations motivate you to act on your deepest desires by boosting your zeal to keep going. They also help you concentrate on fulfilling your goals. They change your negative mindset and self-talk into a positive one while influencing your mind to learn and access new beliefs.

What are these quotes for?

For you.

To let you know you are so much more. To give you strength and the power to be unforgivably you.

Affirmations can bring big transformations into your life by helping make things happen and preventing you from self-sabotaging.

I am not good enough

I can't be in this relationship because

I don't deserve love

I am afraid of

It's too hard

I just can't do it

I am not ready yet

I will never be able to

I suck

Do any or even all of these statements sound familiar?

These are telltale signs of how we often sabotage ourselves through negative self-talk and bring on unnecessary pain and suffering. It makes it much harder to look at ourselves and improve. But that's why this book is here! This book is ready to shove those thoughts out the door and build you back up.

Building your own affirmations

Affirmations are all about changing how you talk to yourself, that is, shifting your negative self-talk to something more positive. Rather than saying I am afraid, say you are fearless. The key to making affirmations powerful is getting the wording right. This way, when you repeat your affirmation over and over again, it becomes a state of mind, a conviction.

Saying uplifting things about yourself helps you feel better and motivates you to reach your goals, increase your self-worth and even help you live a healthier life. Here are a few tips on how to come up with your very own powerful affirmations.

1. Start by picking a negative thought; let's say I am not confident and write its positive opposite. So, in this case, it will be, I am confident.

2. Use "I am" in your affirmations as often as you can; they are extremely powerful words. You are practically telling your mind that you are what you are saying.

3. Use the present tense. Rather than saying I will be confident, say I am confident. This tells your mind that it's not a state you are hoping to achieve in the future, but rather something you have already achieved.

4. Be positive about the wording you use and the thoughts you have. Don't think or talk about what you don't want. For example, I am focusing on what I want because you get what you focus on and what you focus on grows.

5. Be specific, brief, and keep it simple. You want to create an affirmation you can easily remember and something that's not vague.

6. Try to include gratitude in your affirmations. Write them as though you are grateful for already getting or being what you are proclaiming.

7. Lastly, your affirmations should be about yourself and not others; that's why you use the words I am.

Include emotions or feeling words in your affirmations. For example, I am happy with who I am. Here are a few words you can use in your affirmations.

- Amazing

- Enough

- Empowered

- Happy

- Optimistic

- Thankful

- Appreciated

- Energetic

- Harmonious

- Passionate

- Understanding

- Appreciative

- Enthusiastic

- Inspired

- Positive

- Abundant

- Confident

- Excited

- Powerful

- Uplifted

- Courageous

- Expanded

- Joyous

- Proud

- Vibrant

- Creative

- Exuberant

- Lovable

- Radiant

- Vivacious

- Delighted

- Focused

- Loving

- Renewed

- Warm

- Dynamic

- Fortunate

- Luxurious

- Serene

- Wise

- Eager

- Free

- Open Strong

- Worthy

Affirmation list

Now that you know how to come up with your own affirmations, here are a few to get you started. Below is a list of about 50 affirmations for black women.

1. I am Black. I am enough.

2. My friends will have my back.

3. My love is big and my heart is bigger.

4. I will always have a support team.

5. I connect with others on a deeper level.

6. I find strength in vulnerability.

7. It's okay for me to love myself.

8. I am headed in the right direction.

9. By shining my light, I assist others in shining theirs.

10. I don't have to earn my worth.

11. I belong anywhere I go.

12. I focus on what gives me energy. My energy serves as my compass.

13. Being me is how I win.

14. Play is fun, necessary, and restorative.

15. I am my best source of inspiration.

16. I am loved and supported.

17. My self-worth is high.

18. I am creating space for others to show up for me.

19. I am a great version of myself, but I can always make it better.

20. I find new things that I love about myself each day.

21. I am always worthy of success.

22. I can be myself and show others who I am.

23. I love myself as I go through life's changes.

24. I have a support team no matter what I go through.

25. I have a right to feel the way I do.

26. I make sure to grow as I learn from my mistakes.

27. I can speak for myself and say what I need to say.

28. I am stepping into my power.

29. I am focusing on what I want because you get what you focus on and what you focus on grows.

30. I believe in my dreams and let go of my hesitation.

31. I let go of the people who hurt me.

32. I adapt to the situations that come.

33. I find inner peace by doing what I want to do.

34. I work on myself each day even if I don't know it yet.

35. I make the room glow when I enter.

36. No one defines me but me.

37. I need to let go of the past but also learn from it.

38. I take a deep breath before I take the plunge.

39. I am responsible for my success and my failures.

40. I am attracted to what I want by being who I want.

41. I am ready for new experiences, and my soul and being are ready for them.

42. I am energetic when I take on the day.

43. I take each day one step at a time and with determination.

44. I focus on each goal one at a time.

45. I can always be grounded and look for answers.

46. I am clear with my wants and needs.

47. I trust my instincts even when it feels like everything may fall apart.

48. My actions speak louder to those around me.

49. I glow inside and out.

50. I embody things as they should be, not as I want them.

51. I make time for myself to love myself

52. Taking a break is an act of self-compassion.

53. I need rest so I will rest.

54. My mental health is everything to me.

55. I free my time so that I'm not overwhelmed.

56. When I get scared I remind myself that I can hold my own.

57. My work is important but my free time is a must.

58. I can form my own opinions about the world I see.

59. I push back against my anxiety so I can conquer anything.

60. I am fearless.

Here are a few pages for you to list some of your very own affirmations.

_____
_____
_____
_____
_____
_____
_____
_____
_____
_____
_____
_____
_____
_____
_____
_____
_____
_____
_____
_____
_____
_____
_____
_____
_____
_____

How to use this book

These words are meant to help you become the best version of yourself. We will go through various affirmations and even quotes from famous black people about how awesome you are. As black people, they have gone through various struggles much similar to yours and have overcome these obstacles, some even becoming beacons for others, such as yourself, to follow.

You might feel silly saying these affirmations out loud at first, but it will get easier. You might even have trouble saying the words with conviction but consider journaling about your experiences and feelings as you start this journey of change. Try out as many affirmations as you need until you find those that speak to your soul and feel right.

When you start, your inner critic will work really hard to get you to quit by telling you it's a waste of time, but stick with it. After a while, that voice will die down and get replaced by a much kinder one. One that will uplift, support you and have your back. Remember that saying the words is only the first step; you need to follow it up with actions. If you say you are fearless, then do something to confront a fear you have.

Chapter Summary

- The benefits of affirmations can help you daily.

- Repeating these affirmations will help you reaffirm your confidence.

In the next chapter, you will learn how to battle stereotypes.

CHAPTER TWO

The First Fight is the Stereotype

"We must reject not only the stereotypes that others hold of us, but also the stereotypes that we hold of ourselves."

- Shirley Chisolm

Stereotypes

Stereotypes are an uphill battle that you fight daily as a black woman. And one of the biggest reasons for that is chalked up to the media. Let's first start with what the definition of stereotype is.

Stereotypes:

A stereotype is a standardized mental image that some people use

31

to represent an oversimplified opinion, prejudiced attitude, or biased judgement about someone.

Tell me if you've heard some of these phrases before. "Black people love fried chicken. Black people can jump high. All black people are athletic. Black people always commit more crimes."

It hurts to read this because you know it's not true. And the fact that you still have to fight these phrases can be mentally draining and even harmful. I am not athletic, play video games and can't really jump that high, so I don't fit in with these stereotypes and maybe right now you're thinking "Well, I'm not like this," or "Well, I don't do these things," because in reality you are you. These phrases lump you into a group by your skin tone and you have to stand there and go, "But I'm not like this," because you're not.

Luckily we are pushing these stereotypes back. We are saying enough is enough and educating those younger than us on what is right and what is wrong and to treat people equally. And this is where those phrases come in that you can shout to the world

1. I am Black. I am enough.

2. I'm not part of some definition, I like what I like.

3. I belong anywhere I go.

Now, on top of these blatantly false sayings, let's add the fact that you're a woman only adds to this annoying equation. Black women often find themselves having to overcome some widely held stereotypes on their own. She has been told to hide who she is, bleach her skin to be beautiful, get skinnier, control her temper, be less hostile and overly aggressive, just so she can fit in.

Whether it's TV shows, movies, or even social media outlets, the idea that a black woman has to be "sassy" or be looked at as overreacting to valid complaints has long cemented themselves with the large audiences who watch them and are still prevalent to this day. You may feel like your anger is not valid. The same goes for being a woman as well. There are things you may feel are falling down around you, but the moment you say something, it's not taken seriously and you'll either be seen as overreacting or it could be your time of the month. But it's not true. You are voicing your concerns.

What Your Inner Critic Might Say...

Your inner critic might say that it's okay, that these stereotypes are not that bad. They may say that some things are not worth the fight and that you don't want to have trouble in your personal relationships. It's easier to keep your mouth shut and go on with your day.

What You Should Say:

1. "This is not okay."

2. "I do not act like this."

3. "I am just voicing my concern."

4. "I have a right to be angry."

What You Can Do...

Remember that your emotions are valid. If you're angry, then voice that you are angry. If you are upset, voice that you are upset. And if that person is not willing to listen, then find someone who will. You shouldn't have to bend to this idea that the stereotypes set in place are the reasons to stay quiet. You need to be vocal. One of the first ways to break the stereotype is voicing what is and what is not okay.

2. "I'm angry because..."

3. "That is not who I am."

4. "I don't think this can work."

Gatekeeping

Now, aside from the blatant stereotypes that were just talked about, let's also look at gatekeeping. What is it exactly?

Gatekeeping:

Gatekeepers assess who is "in or out."

Gatekeeping is something that not a lot of people think about but happens very often and is in some ways, more subtle. The reason gatekeeping is brought up is because it can make you feel conflicted with your identity. See if this sounds familiar:

"You're not black if you don't like _____"

"You're not black if you can't _____"

"You're not black if you like _____"

If these sound familiar, it's because they're said a lot more often than one would think. The black community is a strong and persevering community, but that doesn't mean you won't face adversity from time to time within that community. Some black women like hip hop, some like classical. Some black women can cook, some black women can't. Some black women believe in God and some don't.

I still remember working my first job and one of my friends was told she's not black because she listens to Demi Lovato and doesn't like rap. It was very weird because some of my other friends were not big on rap and even listened to Japanese punk on occasion. But according to this girl, we weren't black if we didn't like

_____

All of these things, big and small, may be judged from time to time. The idea that you're not black because you don't like what a good portion of black people like can feel like a challenge to your identity. Your inner critic is right there to cement that.

What Your Inner Critic Might Say...

You're not black enough. How can you turn on your community for not liking these things? You don't have an opinion on these issues because you didn't struggle like they did. You're not dark enough. You don't fit in.

What You Should Say:

1.   I am black enough.

2.   No one decides who I am.

3.   No one decides what I like.

4.   Only I can decide who I am and what my passions are.

You are black enough. People tend to forget that black people come from different backgrounds and walks of life. Black people do not all love the same things and have the same hobbies. You are you. Remember that only you can change and be who you want to be.

And above all, it's important to take a deep breath and say what is on your mind. You shouldn't have to face the stereotypes and gatekeeping around you but unfortunately they're there. But fortunately for you, you have your own voice and you can say what you need to say.

Chapter Summary (<u>optional</u>)

Revisit the key points of the chapter in bullet point format. (Example below)

- Stereotypes exist, but they can be broken.

- Stand up to the gatekeepers and do what you want to do.

In the next chapter, you will learn about relationships with others and the power of dating yourself.

CHAPTER THREE

Want Who You Want

"When you love and accept yourself, when you know who really cares about you, and when you learn from your mistakes, then you stop caring about what people who don't know you think."
-Beyoncé Giselle Knowles-Carter

Dating Someone

Dating today can be scary as a woman and a black woman. It's scary because you don't know what to expect. You don't know if they're creepy. You don't know if they're respectful. A lot of dating is through the online world so part of you may take that person's word until you meet in real life. But then let's say you jump through some of the more scary hoops and land someone who makes you happy, something else seems to pop up and get in the way of that happiness. One of the biggest being: What will people think about your partner? What do they do for a living? How do they look? What are their hobbies? All of these things that you are curious about are now asked by everyone around you. Everyone is bombarding you with questions and now it feels like you're being judged for your taste in partners. It can feel overwhelming. So let's look at what the inner critic in you says...

What your inner critic says...

They have to be perfect. People might look down on you if you don't pick the right partner. Will they make you happy? Are you good enough to have a partner? What if that partner doesn't like your friends and family? You are only allowed to date certain people.

What you need to say...

I'm happy being with who I want.

We like different things but we still have a lot of fun.

People do not always get along and that is okay.

I'm good enough to date whoever I want.

People are ready and willing to give their opinions when they are ready. Some opinions show concern for your happiness as well as your safety and wellbeing, and it's okay to take those into account. But understanding which opinions are trivial is important as well. You want to make sure you are separating concerns from blatant judgement so you yourself can be happy. It sounds like a challenge but the end result is your happiness.

So you've finally shifted through the comments and concerns, there might be another challenge ahead, your partner's race. First, understand that you can date whoever you want. If you and that person are comfortable being together then don't let that slip away.

Interracial Dating

You can love whoever you want even if it doesn't feel that way. The idea that you have to date within your race is something that has long been outdated…at least it should be. Don't get me wrong, interracial dating is finally more accepting and public. It's a lot more advertised and shown in different mediums today and it gives hope to the fact that a love like this is being accepted. But what about you? How would your family feel if you fell in love with a non-black person?

For the record, there is nothing wrong with that. But there might be this nagging feeling in the back of your mind because you're worried how other people will respond, especially your family members. I'm bringing this up because I've still seen people make their judgements today. I still remember when my mother was told that she was not allowed to bring a black boy home, and this was in 2014! And then my best friend, who is biracial, has family members who exiled her father because he was marrying a white woman.

It's a stressful thought that shouldn't be stressful, but your family or the public has made it seem like it's something that is almost alien to them. Your inner critic wants to scratch the back of your mind.

Your Inner Critic says…

You shouldn't bring them home. They won't be comfortable. Your family might be angry at you for this. Everyone in your family will have something to say. Are you sure you want to go through that trouble?

What You Should say…

1. Their race does not matter

2. Regardless of whether my family does not approve of their race, they make me happy and that is what is important.

3. We can learn a lot from each other

Going back to the first point, you can date whoever you want and their race may come up in family gatherings but overall if they are making you happy and they make you feel safe, then you are within every right to push back and stand proud with your partner.

Dating Yourself

Now aside from dating someone, you may want a relationship with yourself. It's not the most uncommon thing in the world, sometimes people are simply happier in their own space. But this, like many things, is pushed as a bad thing. You may be in your early 20s or late 40s and there will be people around every corner wondering when you are going to get married. Asking those same pesky kind of questions like is there anyone in your life at the moment? Why not? Are you sure you want to wait to get married? And before you know it, your inner critic is knocking on your door.

Your Inner Critic says…

Are you sure you're happy by yourself? Everyone is right that being alone is really sad. Time is ticking and no one is going to wait around for you forever. No one wants you and that's why you've accepted that you're alone.

What You Should say…

I'm happy by myself.

I will find a partner when I am ready.

I'm learning more about myself and learning how much of a treasure I am.

I don't need someone else to make me happy.

You really can be happy by yourself. One of the greatest things you can do for yourself is learn more about who you are and what you love to do. Being happy by yourself is beneficial as it can be less stressful as well as building self-love. But there are some things to consider if you decide to date yourself.

If you do end up dating yourself, don't forget to take care of yourself. It sounds fairly easy as it's your body, so of course you will! But it takes more work than you think. You need to treat yourself when you can. Take yourself out to dinner, watch a movie, or learn something about yourself. Maybe try a new language or explore a hobby you've always been curious about. Explore the world and show yourself what is out there. Try new foods or grab your friends and go on a little road trip to a state you've always wanted to visit. And don't forget those phrases that we mentioned before.

1. The love I have for myself increases my capacity to love others.

2. Play is fun, necessary, and restorative.

3. I find new ways to come home to myself each day

And one more piece of advice if you have a significant other. You may take care of your partner and let some of your own care slide. Make sure you are also getting that care from them in return. A relationship is a two way street and should be equal in how you treat each other. If you feel you are not being treated equally or not getting the respect you deserve, don't be afraid to leave.

Chapter Summary

Revisit the key points of the chapter in bullet point format.

- Separate your concerns from judgement when it comes to your partner.

- It's okay to be happy by yourself, but make sure you treat yourself every now and then.

- If you have a significant other, don't forget to take care of yourself as well.

In the next chapter, you will learn to speak up for yourself and those around you.

CHAPTER FOUR

Say it Loud!

"The way to right wrongs is to turn the light of truth upon them."
— Ida B. Wells

The Meaning and Importance of Activism

Activism:

The policy or action of using vigorous campaigning to bring about political or social change

It's what pushed the fight for women's rights to do whatever they want just like a man can. Without activism, women would not be able to get an education, have their own career, let alone drive and own a car. The smallest everyday thing that you're able to do would not have happened without the loud and proud voices of feminism and activist. But looking back, black women had to fight harder just to have even remotely the same rights.

Today there may be social issues that you truly care about, one of the most well-known being police brutality. And while there are people of all races standing with you, it may feel like you're a little alone. Some people take activism so far that they try to speak on the behalf of black people when they can very well speak for themselves. This can range from big to small, the biggest being black issues that they don't have experience on, to the smallest of maybe one of your friends arguing for you. It's something that can and can't be ignored. It keeps your voice down when you need to pump it all the way up!

Black Feminism

Black feminism has had its own struggles from the

beginning of feminism to now. Women want to be treated equally but somehow we can't treat each other as such. Black women had to fight not only for their rights for the color of their skin, but then have to fight for rights within their own community for their gender. Even today, many are pulling themselves from "White Feminism," stating that what they were fighting for did not reflect women of color as a whole. On top of that, it's a scary thought when you think of how black women are used as a mouthpiece to speak on topics that don't reflect the majority.

So where do you stand in all of this? Well, if I'm being honest, it's all up to you. If black feminism is your passion, then you will most likely learn more about the history of feminism and how there was a very distinct fight we had to face. On top of that, you may think some things are changing within this active community but at the same time it may feel like some things are still the same. One of the bigger questions you may ask is, what are you fighting for? Well, your inner critic would like to answer those questions and of course they're not very positive.

What Your Inner Critic says…

There's nothing else to fight for. Nothing will change. You contributed to a mostly white pushing movement. Are you even fighting for black women's rights? Clearly not. You abandoned your fellow black sisters to push a white agenda.

What You Should say…

1. I am a Black woman who is fighting for what I believe in.

2. Just because I support the feminist movement doesn't mean I have abandoned my sisters in our fight.

3. I keep myself educated, as my fight is not close to ending.

Overall, this is a subject that has given us the ability to do what we need to do. We can own our own money, market ourselves how we want to and be the boss that we want to be. But where this subject has helped black women, it has also pushed black women to the side. But not anymore. Black women are now speaking up on where they have been pushed to the side or used as that mouthpiece and are pushing back and you should too. Don't forget who you are. Be your own mouthpiece.

White Savior

I'm sure you've heard this term before because it's a behavior that's still alive and kicking. Let's look at the traditional definition first.

White Savior:

The term white savior is a sarcastic or critical description of a white person who is depicted as liberating, rescuing or uplifting non-white people; it is critical in the sense that it describes a pattern in which third world people are denied agency and are seen as passive recipients of white benevolence.

A great example of this would be a movie such as the blindside where a black kid is brought in by a white family and is treated as though he was saved from the inner city streets because he was saved by the white family. They then push those pesky stereotypes about the "hood" and "Black thugs." And then having to push the perspective of white people explaining things to black people who already knew things about said topic.

Another example would be those who volunteer in third world countries to display how charitable they are. The best example of all was Ms. Morello from Everybody Hates Chris, who wanted to truly help her black student. Yet she still holds many racist stereotypes.

Basically it's irritating, it's gross and overall, it's something that needs to be spoken out about because then people get this idea that they too can save the black person from their struggles. And granted that your inner critic might say things that downplay this action

Your Inner Critic Says...

It's not that big of a deal. In this day and age they couldn't possibly get away with advertising something like this on tv. Plenty of people are speaking up for you so you don't need to say anything. Times are changing, things aren't as bad as they used to be so why should I make a fuss. I know they said something because they mean well so I'll just let it go. If anything it's showing that white and black people are working together, so what is the harm?

What You Should Say…

1. I don't need saving

2. This is not okay and needs to be called out

3. This is hurting me more than it's helping me

4. I know you mean well but let me say my piece.

Thanks to the lovely media and entertainment brand we have today, the idea of the white savior is still around and gives people the impression that black people can't help themselves when you know for a fact it's not true. So what do you do? You say it's not okay. You politely point out why it's not okay and why that mentality needs to change. This is also where you repeat some of those lovely phrases from before.

1. My connections with others are steeped in good intentions.

2. I don't have to earn my worth.

3. I am creating space for others to show up for me.

Blackfishing

Now there is something that I want to bring to light that is now catching on but took so long to be criticized. And that my dear reader is the idea of blackfishing. But what is blackfishing?

Blackfishing:

Blackfishing is a type of interpersonal racism that can be harmful, even when a person does not have discriminatory or harmful intentions. This form of racism depicts black people as stereotypes and portrays Black culture as a product.

A great example of this would be celebrities and influencers who claim to be black by either adapting black hairstyles or even darkening their skin so that they can pass as black. It's the newly cosmetic and packaged "blackface." It's now being called out more in recent years and now has a name behind it so that way it can be called out. So what does your inner critic think?

What Your Inner Critic says...

It's not that big of a deal. Others are calling it out so I don't have to. It's a compliment that they want to adopt a black person's look.

What You Should Say...

1. This is insulting and I won't stand for it

2. Here is why this is not okay, it is not your culture.

3. My skin tone is not your fashion product.

It can be frustrating to see those with a huge following be supported for taking on black people's culture and using it to gain attention. It's an insult because they woke up and chose to be black without the racial struggles and the understanding of what it means to be black while you didn't. You as a black woman are someone who is strong with a fire in your heart who didn't choose their skin color but fully embraced it. So what do you do? You tell them it's not okay. Calmly explain to them why it is not okay and bring attention to the issue. Your skin tone is not a fashion product, it is one that holds a long history of oppression and strength and now, freedom.

Fighting Hate with Love

You probably read the title and felt something spark within you. This phrase is all about fighting the hate people have given you over the years for the color of your skin and it's hard to accept that something like this can be possible. I've struggled with this myself, as I have met so many people who look at me as though they can intimidate me because they're a man or because they are white when I was simply trying to work my underpaid job. But the truth is, if we don't put out that love then we will ultimately get nowhere. Your inner critic probably has much to say about this.

What your Inner Critic says…

Why should I even give them the time of day when they

want to be rude and disrespectful? They don't deserve to hear my voice if they're not going to listen. I don't have to endure this hate and they will never learn.

What You Should say…

1. I can be a positive influence and create a change

2. I know people can change but I have to be patient

3. Our generation is learning to be more culturally sensitive and I can help with that.

I'm not saying that you have to forgive the people who have done you wrong. I'm saying that you can educate people on what is right and what is wrong about their behavior and that some people are willing to listen in order to make a difference. If you spew the hate just as they did then you can't rise above and create a bridge of hope for the future under you. By you speaking out and showing that you will give people a chance, you are showing that a connection can be made and that the hate can be broken down.

I can be the change and be loud about what I have to say

You don't have to be active in protests or march every other weekend for what you believe is right. You can simply be vocal in your everyday life with confidence and assertion. Another thing that many black communities are doing is supporting their local black businesses and giving them more attention on social media. Some even spread flyers around their work spaces or give them a quick shout-out whenever they can. You could even raise awareness in your community and do small projects like community gardens. Raise money for inner city children who want to pursue music and arts who may have had their programs shut down.

Change is everywhere and with a simple look around you can show what can be done. Whether you are fighting war on the streets or in the workplace, remember that activism gives you the voice to be loud and proud so don't let people speak for you. Be loud. Be proud.

Chapter Summary

- Black Feminism is important and should not be

forgotten.

- Speak out when someone acts like a white savior.

- Fight hate with love so that you and future generations can make a difference.

In the next chapter, you will learn about inner and outer beauty.

CHAPTER FIVE

Beneath Your Beautiful

"I need to see my own beauty and to continue to be reminded that I am enough, that I am worthy of love without effort, that I am beautiful, that the texture of my hair and that the shape of my curves, the size of my lips, the color of my skin, and the feelings that I have are all worthy and okay."

-Tracee Ellis Ross

Beauty is something that has been radically evolving over the years. It's something that women take pride in and also look to others on what those standards set in place are. The first was the age of modesty where showing your ankles was horrifying and scream-inducing. Then it slowly evolved into showing a little bit of ankle and even some knee, oh my! Then women were finally able to wear pants and you probably get the gist of where this is going. Then there was the subject of weight. Women were having to fight this idea of how beautiful they are based on their weight. You were not allowed to be "fat" and even the ideal weight was always controversial. Then you're not allowed to be skinny or this idea that you were too skinny and needed to put meat on your bones and thicken up.

It's safe to say that all of these thoughts can be a living hell to think about. Black women were having to push through these standards while also trying to be recognized as people alone. The idea of black being beautiful is ever so growing and it's important now more than ever that they express their confidence in how they look.

But like everything is easier said than done. Having self-confidence in how you look will always be an uphill battle. You will have days where you know in your mind that you are ready to shine and then you will have those days where in all honesty you just don't feel great. And that inner critic is more than happy to chime in on this subject.

What your Inner Critic says...

You look like crap. You could take care of yourself but why bother? You're tired. No one cares how you look so why should you? You've gained weight. Your hair is terrible. Your significant other doesn't find you attractive anymore. Do you even have the energy to improve yourself?

What You Should say...

I will not always look great and that is okay.

I am beautiful and comfortable in my own skin.

I can do things to make myself look better and feel better.

Clothes

The first step is clothes. You have to wear them, so why not look good in them as well? But maybe you're not sure what to wear or what your style is. You want to wear something that is comfortable but maybe you also want to look sexy and beautiful. But then when you tried on those clothes, you immediately lost confidence. Don't worry, you're not alone. I have struggled in this boat many times and still do. I remember being upset when I went to a clothing store and getting this icky feeling that I wouldn't look great in anything that I liked. And then my brother charged into the store and was yelling at me to be confident in myself. Oddly enough it worked, but we don't all have brothers who will just yell at us to be confident and try on clothes. That's where your inner thoughts come in to bring you up, right after your inner critic waves at you real quick.

What Your Inner Critic Says…

You won't look good in any of these clothes. That shirt shows off your stomach, and makes you look fat. It looks like you had to go up a size in jeans again, maybe you shouldn't bother. You don't look anything like the girls in the pictures. Your friend said you didn't look great in that outfit you loved so much. Don't show too much or they'll think you're a slut.

What You Should Say…

1. I look good

2. I will dress however I want

3. I will show however much skin I want

You are beautiful in what you wear and if you feel comfortable then no one should take that away from you. You need to yell at yourself and ask yourself why you're upset and then say f*ck that, I look damn good in this outfit! Because you do. And the only one who can take that confidence away and give it back is you. Feel free to pose in the mirror as you find that perfect dress, or those comfortable jeans you always wanted to wear but were too shy to put on. And if you have a little bit of tummy showing, that's okay! Rock the tummy! Don't hide yourself from them.

Makeup

If you're like me and don't wear makeup then this is a

bit of a scary topic as you don't know where to even start. There's so many makeup tutorials but you're not sure which one is the best. Then there is finding your skin tone and then there's trying to apply the correct things to the correct areas. It can be frustrating but if you want to try it then go for it! Makeup is a tool that is empowering and you have every right to try it out, even if your inner critic wants to laugh at you.

What Your Inner Critic Says…

They don't have your skin tone. Your makeup looks bad because you don't know what you're doing. Their makeup looks better than yours because they're wearing famous brands. You can't even afford to look beautiful.

What You Should Say…

1. It may not look amazing now, but I am practicing to make it better.

2. There are more affordable options that will make me look just as good.

3. I have the help of others to master this skill.

Now keep in mind, you don't have to wear makeup to look beautiful as well. Your natural skin shows who you are and the beauty underneath. Whether you wear makeup or not, you are beautiful.

Weight

This is the word we like to avoid, because society has made sure that we take every part of it seriously. As said before, society wants to say many things such as your skinny, too skinny, you're fat, you're not thick enough and you have to sit there and roll your eyes as everyone changes **their** mind about **your** body. The truth is, you can control what you do with your body and if you're at the weight that you like then don't change a damn thing. But if you want to make a change then you can, but it's hard to do. For one, there are too many diets out there that are not that healthy and advise you to starve yourself. Other diets are hard to stick to because they require you to change your eating habits in big ways that you're not used to doing. You don't feel a difference. It can feel demoralizing. Enter your inner critic.

What Your Inner Critic Says…

You can't lose this weight. It will take a lot of effort and energy which you don't even have. They don't find you attractive because of your weight. Are you sure you want to look in the mirror? You're too skinny. You're too fat. Better watch what you eat.

What You Should Say…

1. I can work on my weight but it will take time.

2. I am comfortable in my own skin

3. I will work on myself in my own time and I have people who will support me.

This subject is a hard one to look at because of all of the criticism that comes from others about you. But it's your body and how you treat your body is your decision. If you feel you are having issues with your weight or that you are forming body dysmorphia, make sure you are seeking counseling. It will help you feel better and you won't get hurt getting to the weight that you want. And above all, love yourself. Love who you are. Remember the phrases

1. I make time for myself to love myself.

2. I am headed in the right direction.

3. My greatest glow-up is internal.

There are many different ways that you can make yourself feel better. There are small things like getting your hair done at a salon every now and then. Changing up your look never hurts and clothes are always there to show a new and different kind of you. If you're someone who has never used makeup and wants to try it, then explore. And one more piece of advice, don't forget to build your sisters up. Many black women have to fight these hardships. You're not alone, so don't forget to support your fellow queens and adjust their crowns.

Chapter Summary

- Find clothes and treat yourself when you feel

down.

- Makeup is fun to try. It can also be affordable.

- Weight can always change but make sure you love yourself while you make those changes.

In the next chapter, you will learn about fighting for your dream job.

CHAPTER SIX

Fight Your Fear for that Career

"What's in front of you is a whole world of experiences beyond your imagination. Put yourself, and your growth and development, first"
— Phylicia Rashad

You may be asked at a young age what you want to be when you grow up. The answer comes to you fairly quickly when you're a child because not much thought is given. Of course when you get older, you might change your mind on what you want to be or you simply don't know what you want to be. There are many things that pop up when you try to think about that scary C word. That is why this chapter will break down some fears and misconceptions about finding that dream career.

The Career You Want

The first thing to look at is what do you want to do for a living? What is your passion? What is something you've always wanted to stride to be? It's a scary question that requires you to look inward and open up to your past experiences. Maybe you have given it some thought and you've settled on what you want but it's not a conventional career. These careers would include, but are not limited to: engineer, construction worker, a carpenter, a plumber, etc. Every occupation is uniquely amazing. But your inner critic is knocking on your door with something to say.

What your inner critic says...

You're not as strong as a man so you can't just do what you want. You probably don't even have enough money to go to college and study what you want. It's a tough competition and unfortunately you're not good enough.

Stick to the safe way of doing things. Don't dream too big because then it will end up in disappointment. Do you even need college? Plenty of people turned out just fine. Are you even smart enough to set out to do what you need to do? Even if you get that degree, there's no way you'll get a job in that field.

What you should say...

I can do whatever the hell I want!

I have a passion and I won't let anything get in my way!

There is always a way to reach my goal and I will make it!

If you have a dream, don't let it go. Black women have had to fight to have the same job opportunities as white people. They have had to fight financially to pay for their dream and then fight the biases around them when they want to go into these unconventional jobs. You know you can do these jobs even if it doesn't look like you can. There are many ways to achieve your goal and the route is not always traditional. We live in an age where technology is at our fingertips and can be utilized to get your name out there. If you want to go to college then look for programs that will get you there. Financial aid and scholarships are always there to help boost you up. You may have to work while you're in college and that is okay as well. If you know what you want, then go for it! But remember to research your career and utilize every aid you can.

Fighting for the "Unrealistic Dream"

So what if you want to go the artistic route? You want to be a singer, an artist, a dancer, etc. If you want to grow your own brand, you want to build something from the ground up. But maybe this career path is not as supported because others see your dreams as unrealistic and may even abstain you from doing what you want to. I wanted to be a writer and even talked myself out of going after that career for a long time. I told myself I couldn't make a stable income off of it. After all, more and more people are wanting to grow their own brand or be a writer through the internet as well. And so your inner critic has more than enough to say about it.

What your Inner Critic says...

Do you want to be an artist or a singer? You won't make it past all the others. The competition is too big, you won't possibly be chosen out of everyone else. It's a one in a million chance. School won't help you. You have to get lucky, end of story. Maybe you shouldn't put your work out since no one will like it. You were doomed to fail from the beginning.

What You Should say...

I can get there, I just have to be patient.

I have to get my work out there if I want to make an impact.

I will perfect my craft while I continue to get my name out there.

There are many ways to grow your brand but know that the biggest thing you have to have is patience. Growing a brand and perfecting your art takes time. Sometimes you have to look for the opportunity in order to find your chance to grow. Nothing will happen automatically which is why you have to charge and take that first step. And if you are looking for a job in a certain department, do not get discouraged. The hardest thing I remember coming out of college was finding a job. It was discouraging to see that you either don't have enough years of experience or how you need a master's to get the job you want. But a lot of it was due to me not being patient and building my portfolio later on. Most of all just don't be hard on yourself.

I was at least a little more hopeful when I talked to a career counselor who showed me what people are looking for and even helped me with my resume. Talk to your career counselor as well. This person will offer many resources on how to craft your resume and how to behave during interviews. It gives you a sense of peace. Repeat the following:

1. I inhale my dreams and exhale my fears.

2. My actions match my goals.

3. I accept radical responsibility for creating my dream life.

You're Never Too Old

The final thing to look at is the idea that you maybe hit the age where you think it's too late to follow your dreams. Maybe you're in your mid 40's or late 50's and you still cling to that dream. Maybe you've already retired and think there's no reason to let go of that dream as you had it so long ago. Many of those who retire find work so they can have something to do with their time. If you are within that age range, maybe you want to stay active and do what you couldn't because you financially couldn't at the time. So you decide that you are going to go back to college and pursue your new dreams. You're feeling positive that you can achieve what you set out to do. And no matter what age you are, your inner critic will always be there to remind you of the negatives.

What your Inner Critic says...

That dream was years ago, why would you want to chase after it now? There's no point. It's not like anyone will hire you because of your age. You're not really thinking about going back to school, are you? No one will take you seriously.

What You Should say...

1. I can achieve my dreams, it just may be a later age than I thought.

2. It's never too late for me to get the education I want.

3. I never let my dream go and because of that I'll keep striving even as I age.

That second phrase is the truest. it's never too late to go back and get your education. Older students are always prevalent and if you are someone who was unable to get your GED, it's not too late as well. My mother worked in medical records for over ten years and hated what she was doing. When I turned 18 and was out of the house, she decided it was finally time to study what she wanted to do and what she wanted to do was welding. So she went back to school at the age of 44 and got her degree and was then hired just a few months later as a welder and was melding car pieces. The point is, she never thought she was too old to chase after your dreams and neither should you. We have been pushed by this idea that we have to get that dream job by the time we hit our mid 20's. We have to do something grand and amazing and if we don't do it by the time we are 30, it's all downhill. But that's not true. If you want to study an art, it's never too late to do so. No matter what age you are, you can strive for that career and change your future as you see fit.

Chapter Summary

Revisit the key points of the chapter in bullet point format. (Example below)

- Explore what you want to do and research your career options.

- If you want to grow your brand, look for opportunities to do so and remember that patience is a great key to your success.

- You're never too old to get your degree and learn something new.

In the next chapter, you will learn the idea of family.

CHAPTER SEVEN

What Family Means

"Talk about your negative experiences with the father, with your girlfriends. Not with your children. And bite your tongue when it comes to diminishing, denying, dismissing, name-calling."
-Iyanla Vanzant

What does family mean exactly? What makes a family? It's probably not a question you'd ask in your everyday life. Well, let's start with a definition. If we look at the most simplistic definition of family, it may read something like this:

A group of one or more parents and their children living together as a unit.

While the definition reads as a unit consisting of parents and children, we know that it goes much deeper than that. Family comes in different shapes and forms and overall is what can bring you up when you are at your lowest. It's what built your values and nurtured you over time, but like many others, you may not have grown up in that traditional definition. Your family could have been chaotic or broken but now it's healing. There are times where you want to have your say and release what you have held onto for so long. You may have a much more different definition of family and may even have conflicts you want to resolve. Well, that's what this chapter is all about! It's time for you to put your foot down. If you're not sure where to start don't worry, this chapter is here for that as well. So let's run through ideas and familial conflicts that you may face.

Forming Your Own Values

The first is family values and the idea of politics and personal beliefs. You were taught at a young age that doing the wrong thing can lead to consequences and that you morally should not act on that bad behavior. For instance you were taught not to lie, not to steal, be polite and so on. You may have even grown up with a heavy religious background. Many of those values come from a higher being. There is nothing wrong with that. But when you get older, you begin to think for yourself. When doing so, you begin to form your own opinions. This is great because you explore yourself and the world! But your family opposes your beliefs. Your inner critic would like to have a word with you.

What your Inner Critic says...

What if your family over reacts? You should keep your mouth shut so that you don't cause any trouble. Maybe they'll talk about you behind your back. They could shut you out if you don't agree.

What You Should Say...

1. I can think for myself.

2. I won't go back on my beliefs and my own values.

3. I will be outspoken if need be, otherwise you can

believe what you believe.

Your family will not always agree and if you want to keep your opinions to yourself then do that. It's all about your comfortability. But if you feel that you need to be outspoken, don't be afraid to speak your mind. Sit down with your family and have a discussion on what you've learned. But know that you shouldn't be silenced to appease others, including family members.

Friends are Family

Like I said, everyone has a different definition of family. Some don't have parents and some see their friends as family members or even prefer them over their own family members. I grew up always wanting a sister and my best friends have been just that for over 20 years. I even introduced her as my sister and instead of my best friend. If you have someone like that too, then you understand the value of having someone so close to you that they are better than blood. But you might take issue with this definition of family. For one, maybe your family has turned their back on you and your friends were the only ones you had to turn to. Maybe they took you in because your family kicked you out. Or sometimes your friends tend to get too close and also expect a lot from you. But then you try to mend those family ties and make it clear that your friends have been there for you. Maybe it is time for you to return the favor and your family wants you to prioritize your time with them. And while they're pulling you back and forth, your inner critic joins in the tug of war.

What Your Inner Critic Says…

You should feel guilty for not always helping them when they ask you to. Your family is related to you. Your friend is not part of your own flesh and blood. You should tell them everything because they helped you when you needed it most. You shouldn't prioritize your friends over your family.

What You Should Say…

1. My friends are my family

2. I will be there for those who have been there for

me.

3. Though I care about my friends and family, I will also care about myself and be there for them when I can.

You shouldn't have to pick between your friends and your family but like you've maybe heard a dozen times, no family is perfect. Neither friend is perfect. It's okay to see your friends as family and choose those friends over family. Your family consists of the people who have been there for you the most. They are the ones that held you when you cried. They are the ones that are rooted in your success. They will be there as you experience life, even if they are far away.

Your Own Family Values

You are now the new parent of your pride and joy and you might be in panic mode because you don't know what to do. You're looking at books, you're watching videos, you're doing all the research you can to make sure your child makes it past the age of three. But overall, as your child gets older, you get into the swing of things and you know what you want to teach your child. As said before, you grew up with your own values and beliefs and you want your child to learn these things as well. But then you are being looked at and judged by everyone around you. Your family has values that they want to teach them and then you have the public wanting to teach your child whatever they want as well. But your inner critic wants to give you some critiques as well

What Your Inner Critic Says…

You're not ready to be a mother. What if you screw up? Maybe you should just let your family teach them what you need since you don't know what you're doing. Are you even financially ready to have this child? You're not going to be able to give them everything. Are you sure you even want to be a mother? What if they make the same mistakes you did?

What You Should Say…

1. I will be a great mother

2. No parent is perfect and I will make mistakes

3. I will love my child and teach them the best I can

It's scary to think about being a mother and it's scary to think about the ways you might mess up. But it's great to have the confidence that you will love your child no matter what and will teach them right from wrong. It's okay to let your family teach them their values as well but make sure that you are putting your foot down when they overstep.

The Talk

If you read these two words then you probably know what this section is about. It's about how to explain to your children how to act in public and around the police. Many black families have to go through this same talk and have carried this heavy weight with them for generations. Big things such as how to act in public, how to act when pulled over by the police and to be careful if you drive or walk through a white neighborhood. These topics are scary to teach your child. As much as you hope these talks can stop one day, we're still not there yet. Your inner critic is there to stoke your fears.

What Your Inner Critic Says...

Will I tell them everything they need to know? Will they miss anything? What if they do get profiled? Will they be okay? Will they get justice if something goes wrong? What if I lose them to police brutality?

What You Should Say...

1. I will teach them everything I can so that they don't meet a quick fate.

2. I will fight with all my might to make sure my kids get justice.

3. I will be outspoken on this matter and will refuse to stay quiet.

This is not an easy section to read. It's scary, it's horrifying, and it's something that will not go away anytime soon. But that is why it's important to speak out on these kinds of topics. It's not all doom and gloom as the black community is doing everything they can to let these behaviors be known so that there can be some form of change. For a new mother, this talk does not get easier. But it's good to be truthful with them. Make sure you share your experiences with them and make sure your family shares their stories as well. Teach them to do research on the matter by looking up different ways black people have had their interactions and what they can do to stay safe. Remember that you are a strong black woman who will speak up and protect what is right.

Your Support System

Last but not least, let's talk about your support system. You want to make sure you are surrounded by people who will bring you up when you are feeling down. Sometimes your inner voice won't feel like enough and it helps to have those outer voices remind you that you are awesome and that you can do anything! It even helps that you surround yourself with voices that speak on the strength of black women in this country. But your inner critic wants to block those voices out so they can replace them with their own.

What Your Inner Critic Says...

You don't have a support system. I'm bothering people. I can handle everything on my own. I don't need anyone else to look after me. I don't need to ask for help.

What You Should Say...

1. It's play to ask for help

2. I can't handle everything on my own and that is okay.

3. I am still independent while I am also loved.

It is okay to have a support system. It is okay to ask for help. It is okay to be loved and put trust in those around you because it helps to be told you are loved and supported. Because you are loved and supported whether it is by your family, friends, or even the community around you. You are loved and let's not forget those wonderful phrases from chapter one.

1. I am loved and supported.

2. I can be myself and show others who I am.

3. I don't need all the answers to remain grounded at this moment.

Chapter Summary

- It is okay to be outspoken with your family on what you truly believe.

- Friends are just as important as family and can even be thicker than blood.

- If you are a new mother, do not be afraid as you will be amazing.

- The "Talk" is an important one to have and needs to be treated with care.

- A support system is always important.

In the next chapter, you will learn self-respect.

CHAPTER EIGHT

R-E-S-P-E-C-T

"We all require and want respect, man or woman, black or white. It's our basic human right."
—*Aretha Franklin*

Respect is something that is earned and given by everyone around you. It's something that you give back if you deem them worthy of it. It's something that can also be lost due to time, screw ups and overall attitude. Black women have demanded respect just for being a human being. Giving that respect to others is much harder than people think. In this final chapter, I want you to look inward at your self-respect. It's hard to use that word if you don't respect and take care of yourself. You don't want to be a doormat. You don't want to be walked on and you don't want people thinking they can walk all over you because you're a black woman who might get angry and give them a show. There is a word that is going to pop up a lot and the word is "Toxic." I'm sure you've heard it before. This chapter is going to work a little differently. For this one, we are going to look at what defines a toxic relationship and look at what questions you should ask yourself. If you are saying yes to some of these questions, then it will be time to look even deeper at yourself and how you can improve or drop the relationship. And in case you were curious, yes, your inner critic will be there to criticize you while you ask yourself these questions. But like every other chapter before, we have the words that will slice them in half!

The first thing we need to look at is, what is the definition of toxic?

Toxic:

A toxic person is anyone whose behavior adds negativity and upset to your life.

With this definition, let's run through different examples of people you need to let go.

Toxic Friends

Friends are family, just as we mentioned in the last chapter, but should some of your friends be your family? You've known this person for so long that you may not recognize some habits they have produced. Or if you have recognized these habits, maybe you shrugged them off because you're used to their actions. So the first few questions you should ask yourself is, are their traits toxic? So do they...

1. Only call you when you need something but don't answer when you need something?

2. Are your conversations equal when you talk to them? Do they ask how you are doing and listen to you or are they only speaking about themselves and their struggles? Are they asking if you are okay?

3. When something good happens to you, do they make it about themselves?

4. Do they use your secrets and flaws against you? Do they use them to make you do what they want

or remind you of your screw-ups so that you are guilted into going along with what they want to do?

5. Do they talk about you to your face and embarrass you publicly, or do they talk behind your back? Do they bad-mouth you to your other friends?

6. Do they get you in trouble and then bail when you need them the most?

7. Do they exclude you from hangouts with your mutual friends?

If you are saying yes that they do have these negative traits then it's time you sit them down and have a conversation about it. You have to put your foot down and calmly lay out why these behaviors are not acceptable and that you should have more respect from them. If you're scared to have this conversation, it's more than likely that your inner critic is trying to salvage a possibly ending friendship.

What Your Inner Critic Says…

They have been your friends for years, and you want to

change that? They're right, that you are overreacting to something so small just because they decided to make it about themselves this one-time. What about all the good things they did for you? You've already helped them out so many times, what's not one more? You said you would always be there for them, are just going to break your promise like that?

What You Should Say...

1. I deserve friends who will have my back.

2. I shouldn't feel bad about myself anytime we hang out together.

3. I deserve to be respected.

All of those statements are more than true. You deserve respect and you shouldn't feel guilted into hanging out with your friend or even doing them a favor. And that is why, like I said before, you should sit them down and explain what they are doing wrong. And how they react should tell you if you just need to drop them. If they choose to blame you and pull up all of your shortcomings just as they said before, then they are not worth keeping. They've already talked down to you so many times before and you don't need them to do it now. If they agree that they need to change, then give them a chance. If they do not improve, then sever your ties. You deserve people who love you.

Toxic Relationships

This one can be scary. For one, black women are not as praised for leaving their toxic partners as white women are. Many are scared to call the police because they don't want themselves or their partner to be another statistic. On the other side of wanting to leave your partner, you may have missed signs of what an abusive and toxic relationship looks like. I was in one for five years. I wasn't physically abused, but I was verbally abused. I was scared to argue or fight back whenever they got angry with me. Part of the reason I didn't leave was because I didn't realize what kind of relationship I was in. It wasn't until I talked to a therapist years later that they were able to point out the harsh behaviors. So let's first look at the signs of an abusive and toxic relationship.

1. Are they extremely jealous? Do they show up randomly or call you constantly asking you where you are? Are they always trying to keep you from going out with friends?

2. Are they controlling? Do they ask what you're doing with your money? Do they make you ask if it's okay to go out even to simple places like the grocery store? Do they try to control everything financially?

3. Are they blaming you or everything else whenever something happens to them? It could be completely unrelated to you, but somehow you're to blame.

4. Do they force themselves on you sexually or grow angry when you are not in the mood or say no?

5. Are they verbally abusive and call out so many parts of your appearance or compare you to all of these other women?

6. Do they violently or non-violently threaten you with physical violence?

7. Do they have sudden mood swings from caring to hateful?

Some of these actions are easily spotted and some are not until it's too late. These are behaviors you need to get away from because in the end, these types of people don't change. And your inner critic is there, trying to change your mind.

What Your Inner Critic Says…

I can fix them. I can make them better, they just need a little patience. It was a one-time thing, I'm sure they won't do it again. They're just in a bad mood, I should just leave them alone for now. Maybe it is my fault that they are not happy, I need to be better. They said they have changed, and they seem sincere. Maybe I should get back together with them. They promised they would never hurt me again and that they'll even treat me better.

What You Should Say…

1. They will not change

2. I am worth so much more than this

3. It's not my fault and I can leave this

4. I am strong and I am brave and I will be okay

As I said before, black women are a lot less praised for leaving their spouses or partners but that doesn't mean they are alone. There are support systems in place for black women so that they can feel safe. Some of these organizations include

Blackburn Center

National Coalition Against Domestic Violence

National Coalition of 100 Black Women and NCBW

There are resources out there for black women to get help in leaving these relationships. If you are worried that you are in danger, gather your support systems. While you handle these relationships, don't forget these phrases.

1. I prioritize my peace.

2. I am fearless

3. I honor my commitment to take care of myself.

Breaking the Stigma

This section wants you to respect your mind. Your mental health is a great part of your self-respect. Your mental health is how you will handle the world around you and how you will handle your personal relationships. It's not a popular opinion in the black community to seek mental health resources and it's time to break that stigma. This is also where your support system comes in and brings you up when you are feeling down. At times, everything feels like it is crashing down. But you can pull yourself back up.

What Your Inner Critic Says...

You're crazy and that's why you need to talk to a therapist. What if you have to take pills? Everyone will judge you for doing so. You won't have the support you think you do. Black people don't get mental health, we keep it to ourselves like we should. Everyone else struggles and they're not getting help so why do you need to? How is a stranger going to solve all of my problems? You're clearly not strong enough to handle everything on your own, are you sure a therapist will really help you solve your problems?

What You Should Say...

1. It's okay to ask for help.

2. I know what I need and my friends will have my back.

3. It's okay if I have to take medication because I will feel better.

This stigma needs to be broken. If you are not feeling mentally well then do not hesitate to get help. People's opinions are not worth suffering on the inside. You are wonderful and you will be okay. You respect yourself by taking care of yourself mentally and physically.

Chapter Summary

- Don't let toxic friends walk all over you and let

them know their behavior is bad.

- You deserve a loving partner. You can get away from abusive relationships. There are resources for black women to get the help they need.

- Your mental health is important and you deserve to have a healthy mind and seek out a professional.

Final Words

You are beautiful and Black, and there's nothing wrong with that. You are strong and brave and kind and outspoken. You are all of these things and you can't let anyone tell you differently. Your struggles are different and though the world is learning it's not where it needs to be when trying to understand black women.

Remember to skip to each chapter for whatever you need and remember that these chapters are here to help you and reaffirm who you are. You should fight stereotypes and gatekeeping. You should be able to date who you want to date or be happy by yourself. You should be loud in how you feel and call out these white savior complexes. You should feel beautiful and try new things. You should fight for the career you want. You should have the family you want. You should have the self-respect that you deserve.

But you won't always feel that way. You won't always feel outspoken and beautiful and your inner critic will never fully leave you because it's a part of you. But you can say that I am enough. You can say that I deserve to be loved and respected. That is why you have a list of phrases to repeat throughout the book. Because none of these phrases are lies. They are simply the truth.

I hope you treasure this book and find something meaningful and helpful. I hope you are reaffirming these phrases in your everyday life and are succeeding. Because to repeat what I've said before one more time:

You are beautiful, you are Black, and there's nothing wrong with that.

Thank You

Before you leave, I'd just like to say, thank you so much for purchasing my book.

I spent many days and nights working on this book so I could finally put this in your hands.

So, before you leave, I'd like to ask you a small favor.

Would you please consider posting a review on the platform? Your reviews are one of the best ways to support indie authors like me, and every review counts.

Your feedback will allow me to continue writing books just like this one, so let me know if you enjoyed it and why. I read every review and I would love to hear from you.

To leave a review simply go to Amazon.com, go to "Your Orders" and then find it under "Digital Orders".

References

20 Inspirational Quotes For Black Moms and Their Daughters (From Oprah, Maya Angelou, and More!) (2016, February 18th) Black News.com. https://blacknews.com/news/inspirational-quotes-for-black-moms-daughters-from-maya-angelou-oprah-more/

BOTWC Staff (2020, November 3rd). REMEMBERING SHIRLEY CHISHOLM: THE FIRST BLACK WOMAN TO RUN FOR PRESIDENT FOR THE DEMOCRATIC PARTY. Because We Can. https://www.becauseofthemwecan.com/blogs/botwc-firsts/remembering-shirley-chisholm-the-first-black-woman-to-run-for-president-for-the-democratic-party

Evans, Erin. (2022). 33 Beyoncé Knowles Quotes About Confidence and Finding Your Self-Worth. BrightDrops.com. https://brightdrops.com/beyonce-knowles-quotes

Graham. C. Toni (2022). Toni's Talk. https://www.goodreads.com/quotes/844041-toni-s-talk-when-you-invest-in-yourself-you-have-instant

NYPL Staff. (2018, July 18th) The Way to Right Wrongs: Celebrating the Legacy of Ida B. Wells. NYPL.org. https://www.nypl.org/blog/2018/07/16/way-right-wrongs-celebrating-legacy-ida-b-wells

Peters, Terri (2021, January 29th) 21 inspiring quotes celebrating Black history to share with your kids. Today.com. https://www.today.com/parents/21-black-history-quotes-share-your-kids-today-t207446

Sparks, Abbe (2020, August 16th) ARETHA FRANKLIN ON RESPECT FOR HUMAN RIGHTS: QUOTE OF THE WEEK. Socially Spraked News. https://sociallysparkednews.com/aretha-franklin-respect-for-human-rights-quote-of-the-week/

Weatherford, Ashley (2016, March 18th) Tracee Ellis Ross Wants To Make TV That Reflects Black People's Real Lives. The CUT. https://www.thecut.com/2016/03/tracee-ellis-ross-race-blackish-black-girls-rock.html

www.ingramcontent.com/pod-product-compliance
Lightning Source LLC
Chambersburg PA
CBHW031434120626
46545CB00006B/2403